SWITCHING SYSTEMS

LEON MCDONALD, III

Published by So It Is Written, LLC
Rochester, MI
SoItIsWritten.net

Switching Systems

Edited by: So It Is Written – www.SoItIsWritten.net

Formatting: Ya Ya Ya Creative – YaYaYaCreative@gmail.com

ISBN: 979-8-9993606-3-2

LCCN: 2025917257

PRINTED AND BOUND IN THE UNITED STATES OF AMERICA

Table of Contents

Introduction 1

The Perfect Position 5

Survival Mode vs. Dream Mode 11

The Call For More 15

Applying Pressure 19

Flipping The Switch 31

Put God In The Game 39

Switching Mindsets 41

Areas To Shift Your Mind 45

Switching Systems Requires Spiritual Maturity 55

The Posture of The Mature 59

Worship and Impatience 61

Switching Languages 63

Get An Interpreter 67

Hide-and-Seek 73

Watch Your Mouth 77

Talk Your Way Out 79

Switch Relationships 83

The Power of The Right People and The Right Words . . 87

Living by Believing 91

About The Author 95

Introduction

>>>━━━◆ ⋯ ⋅ ◆ ⋯ ◆━━━━<<<

*A*t the beginning of each year, The Winners Circle Church and I dedicate an entire week to our spiritual health. As we commence on this seven-day journey, we set our hearts toward seeking God's plan and vision for the year ahead. This time of intense prayer, worship and revelation has often been referred to as *consecration*.

During this time of amplified pursuit, our church gathers daily to experience the presence of God, listen for direction and plan for the future. Many parishioners look forward to this experience every year and it never fails to deliver. The sense of expectancy in the room is palpable and the atmosphere is electric. Each encounter is unique, and every moment carries heightened anticipation. As soon as you step onto the property, you sense the life-giving, life-changing energy of God flowing.

As I was praying over the theme for 2022, Holy Spirit dropped two words in my spirit: *switching systems*! These simple words would be the catalyst for unleashing the power of God in the lives of countless people. Those words pack incredible power. Switching systems was an experience at our local church, but it has since turned into an avalanche in the body of Christ.

Let's be clear. This is not just a book. It is a transformative resource. It's a movement. You are reading the blueprint that will strategically help you tap into a level of living you never thought possible. It is my prayer that this blueprint will shift your life forever.

God is doing something supernatural for you. Oftentimes, we are so concerned about the wellbeing of others that we neglect ourselves. But as you venture through this book, I pray God touches you. I am in faith that you will have a personal experience with God just like we did during those 7 days. My heart's desire is to see you change the way you think and, therefore, change the way you live. Switching systems is an instrument from the heart of God to help you produce meaningful results. Therefore, I am praying that these pages inspire, empower and equip you to operate and live in a new way.

This is a call to the hungry, the thirsty and the determined. It is a summons to the sensitive. to go deeper and search for more. This resource beckons you to reflect the passion of the psalmist in Psalms 42:1-2 (AMP): *As the deer pants [longingly] for the water brooks, so my soul pants*

*[longingly] for you, O God. My soul (my life, my inner self)
thirsts for God, for the living God.*

I know you are ready for more. You know there is more.
Your investment in this tool validates that truth. Take a deep
breath. Prepare to leave everything you know, and you think
you know, behind. A new you with accelerated results and
uncommon outcomes lies ahead. But it requires a switch.

So, get ready to *switch systems*!

Notes & Reflections

The Perfect Position

*P*hilippians 3:13 (NLT) says, *No, dear brothers and sisters, I have not achieved it, but I focus on this one thing: Forgetting the past and looking forward to what lies ahead...*

Luke 5:37-38 (HCSB) says, *And no one puts new wine into old wineskins. Otherwise, the new wine will burst the skins, it will spill, and the skins will be ruined. But new wine should be put into fresh wineskins.*

> ... possessing something new requires releasing something old.

Philippians 3:13 teaches us about forgetting what is behind and reaching for what is ahead. I honestly believe possessing something new requires releasing something old. Luke 5:37-38 highlights how dangerous it is to place new wine in old wineskins. In fact, it's actually considered wasteful to behave in this manner. Holy Spirit is prompting many of you right now to reflect, re-think and re-imagine. What must you release to move forward? How are you going to stretch, press and reach for what is ahead?

The thought of letting go can be hard. That's where the power of Holy Spirit comes to the rescue.

Two metaphors have been used throughout Scripture to describe the nature and character of Holy Spirit: fire and water. First, let's examine fire. Fire is powerful. It can be extremely destructive. But the truth is, in order to move ahead, certain mindsets, attitudes and behaviors must be destroyed. As you begin the journey to *Switching Systems*, prepare for Holy Spirit to set some stuff on fire. I decree that God is even beginning to burn up any and everything that stands in the way of your progress.

On one hand, fire is a metaphor for the consuming power of Holy Spirit. But fire also speaks to giving life and spirit to. It means to fill with enthusiasm and passion. It signifies an explosion. God wants to fill you with passion. He wants to ignite your life by way of Holy Spirit. It is my prayer that you would open your heart and let God set you on fire. I intercede for you and ask Holy Spirit to set a fire down in your soul that cannot be contained or controlled.

Another metaphor for the Holy Spirit is water. Similar to fire, water can be beneficial in certain aspects, yet destructive in others. Consider individuals impacted by flooding due to a hurricane or powerful storm. The volume and force of the water destroys everything in its path. With the image of a flood in mind, consider my next statement.

God has a plan to flood every enemy force that has been dispatched against you.

In Exodus 14, the children of Israel encounter a miracle through the hand of God. They cross The Red Sea on dry ground. But interestingly enough, Pharoah, his army and chariots try and cross over, too. Let's pick the story up in verse twenty-three.

Exodus 14:23-28:

Then the Egyptians pursued them into the middle of the sea, even all Pharaoh's horses, his war-chariots and g his charioteers. So it happened at the early morning watch [before dawn], that the LORD looked down on the army of the Egyptians through the pillar of fire and cloud and put them in a state of confusion. He made their chariot wheels hard to turn, and the chariots difficult to drive; so the Egyptians said, "Let us flee from Israel, for the LORD is fighting for them against the Egyptians."

When all the Israelites had reached the other side, the LORD said to Moses, "Raise your hand over the sea again. Then the waters will rush back and cover the Egyptians and their chariots and charioteers." So as the sun began to rise, Moses raised his hand over the sea, and the water rushed back into its usual place. The Egyptians tried to escape, but the LORD swept them into the sea. Then the waters returned and covered all the chariots and charioteers—the entire army of Pharaoh. Of all the Egyptians who had chased the Israelites into the sea, not a single one survived.

There are so many themes to consider in this passage, but let's quickly examine a few. First, we see God making it difficult for the enemy to operate against the people of God. We live in a world where it seems like evil is multiplying at an accelerated pace. When we turn on the television or view the latest trending social media post, it seems like the enemy is having his way. But we can build our faith on Exodus 14. Although opposition is present, we see a God with power to disrupt demonic plans. Our God has a history filled with supernatural intervention and displays of His divine ability. God's resume is undeniable, with unlimited references to support it. Therefore, I pray things get easier for you, yet more challenging for your adversaries.

Next, we see God bring closure and resolution to the problem the children of Israel were facing. He did not just make it difficult for the enemy; God *drowned* them. This passage of Scripture provides hope. It demonstrates we can trust that God will not leave loose ends. He finishes what He starts.

Hebrews 10:23 (KJV) says, *Let us hold fast the profession of our faith without wavering, for he is faithful that promised.*

Hebrews 10:23 (AMP) says, *Let us seize and hold tightly the confession of our hope without wavering, for He who promised is reliable and trustworthy and faithful [to His word].*

If you find yourself currently in the middle of a storm or something challenging, stand firm, knowing God is not done. You are in perfect position for an Exodus 14 experience. You are about to see every one of your personal Pharaohs drowned in the presence of God. Your current struggle is being handled by the power of a loving father. As you switch systems, the devil is not going to make it through the transition.

Notes & Reflections

Survival Mode vs. Dream Mode

*S*witching systems is about adjusting the way you live. For many, the thought of operating differently brings trepidation. Let's be honest. Change can be disorienting. But I assure you that once you make the switch, you will never want to return to the way things used to be.

Through switching systems, God is moving you from survival mode to dream mode. This is a monumental shift. Survival mode is all about maintaining what you have. It screams safe! The only issue is "safe" does not create. Safe does not get paid. If you want to go where others have not gone, you must do what others will not do. We must leave survival mode and switch to dream mode. When we flip that switch, we answer the call of God to live based on what He can do.

Leaving survival mode is a liberating, limit-breaking decision. As you switch to dream mode, you are no longer confined by budgets, resources, timelines or past mistakes. In this mode, your only confinement is your own imagination. It is from this perspective that God created the world, and you are about to create, too!

Genesis 1:1-5 (MSG) says:

First this: God created the Heavens and Earth—all you see, all you don't see. Earth was a soup of nothingness, a bottomless emptiness, an inky blackness. God's Spirit brooded like a bird above the watery abyss. God spoke: "Light!" And light appeared. God saw that light was good and separated light from dark. God named the light Day, he named the dark Night. It was evening, it was morning—

Day One.

God looked over the void and dark world and saw what it could be. He saw light before light materialized. Light existed on the canvas of God's imagination before it appeared in the natural. God saw light in dream mode. Then, what God saw in dream mode, he spoke into being. This same power to create resides in you. What will you see? What can you imagine? What could it be?

Genesis 1:26-28 (MSG) says:

God spoke: "Let us make human beings in our image, make them reflecting our nature So they can be responsible for the fish in the sea, the birds in the air, the cattle, And, yes, Earth itself, and every animal that moves on the face of Earth." God created human beings; he created them godlike, Reflecting God's nature. He created them male and female. God blessed them: "Prosper! Reproduce! Fill Earth! Take charge! Be responsible for fish in the sea and birds in the air, for every living thing that moves on the face of Earth."

You have been created in the image of God. You reflect God's nature, and you have been given responsibility for the earth. Your life, family, business, church, ministry and finances are under your authority. With the godlike creativity you have been given, speak to them. In dream mode, you accept God's charge to Prosper, Reproduce, Fill the Earth and Take Charge!

> You are not looking for an answer; you *are* the answer.

Dream mode takes you off the sidelines and puts you in the game. You are not looking for an answer; you are the answer. As you switch from survival mode to dream mode, get ready to declare, "Life is good!"

Regain Your Appetite

If you have ever been sick, you know what it means to lose your appetite. Through the fatigue and discomfort of constant coughing, sneezing and a sore throat, eating seems to be the farthest thing from your mind. Sometimes your stomach aches and is uneasy. There may also be apprehension in eating because of the fear that it may come back up. You know eating is necessary to maintain strength and fuel the immune system to fight; yet, it remains challenging to do so.

Look at this situation from a spiritual perspective. We know we should read the Word, pray consistently and worship daily. Yet, we find it difficult to implement. Oftentimes, it is the infections from life that leave us weak and fatigued. Trust me. I can relate to your experience. But I am praying that you get your appetite back. As you navigate this resource, your desire for God will intensify. Your strength will return. Your appetite for the things of God will become insatiable. The question will not be if you want to eat, but *how much* you can eat.

The Call For More

>>►—————•••◆ · · · ◆ · · · ◆•••————•‹‹‹

$\mathcal{R}$ecently, I began a devotional by Former NFL coach Tony Dungee. The book is called *The Uncommon Life*. In one of the excerpts, he said, "You not only have faith, but you are called to faith." This statement captivated me. It spoke to the concept of not just possessing faith. It uncovered the idea that God will pull us into faith.

Romans 1:17 (KJV) says, *"...the just shall live by faith"* and *"the righteousness of God is revealed from faith to faith."*

The journey with God is not static; it's dynamic. We are constantly being pulled out of one place into another. Faith challenges who we are to transform us into who we should be.

> You will never walk by faith and end up empty-handed.

God's call to faith is a call for more. The birth of a dream on the inside is a divine invitation to leave where we are and venture to a new place. Listen closely. Whenever God calls you to faith, it is because He wants to give you something.

You will never walk by faith and end up empty-handed. God is calling you to a place called *more*. Will you answer?

> John 10:10 (MSG) says, *A thief is only there to steal and kill and destroy. I came so they can have real and eternal life, more and better life than they ever dreamed of.*

> John 10:10 (AMP) says, *The thief comes only in order to steal and kill and destroy. I came that they may have and enjoy life, and have it in abundance [to the full, till it overflows].*

There is an abundant, overflowing life awaiting you. You were not created to *endure* life. Instead, you were designed to *enjoy* life. As you switch systems, embrace the idea that life is going to be better than you have ever dreamed.

Where do I begin?

The place called *more* sounds enticing. But that is where the questions start flowing. How do I get there? What do I need to do? Where do I begin?

Good questions. The starting point to more is the Word of God and obedience.

> Hebrews 11:3 (KJV) says, *"Through faith we understand that the worlds were framed by the word*

of God, so that things which are seen were not made of things which do appear."

We learn from this passage that the Word of God should create our world. When we receive the Word, either written or spoken, we are being given the building blocks for our future. The Word of God becomes the substance and material that creates the preferred outcomes we seek. The journey to more begins with hearing what God *has* said and *is* saying.

After God gives us His Word, He is looking for obedience. The Word in 1 Samuel 15:22 (NLT) says, *But Samuel replied, "What is more pleasing to the LORD: your burnt offerings and sacrifices or your obedience to his voice? Listen! Obedience is better than sacrifice, and submission is better than offering the fat of rams."*

> When the Word meets obedience, overflow happens.

When the Word meets obedience, overflow happens. You will never find overflow when there is not a Word from God or obedience from a person. First, God gives His Word. Next, we align our actions with the Word by faith. When these two steps are completed, the result is more than enough. Never forget that abundance follows obedience.

Notes & Reflections

Applying Pressure

>⟩⟩→────•◆ · · • ◆ • · · ◆•───◄◄⟨

*L*uke 23:13-23 (HCSB) says:

Pilate called together the chief priests, the leaders, and the people, and said to them, "You have brought me this man as one who subverts the people. But in fact, after examining Him in your presence, I have found no grounds to charge this man with those things you accuse Him of. Neither has Herod, because he sent Him back to us. Clearly, He has done nothing to deserve death. Therefore, I will have Him whipped and then release Him." For according to the festival he had to release someone to them.

Then they all cried out together, "Take this man away! Release Barabbas to us!" (He had been thrown into prison for a rebellion that had taken place in the city, and for murder.)

Pilate, wanting to release Jesus, addressed them again, but they kept shouting, "Crucify! Crucify Him!" A third time he said to them, "Why? What has this man done wrong? I have found in Him no grounds for the death penalty. Therefore, I will have Him whipped and then release Him." But they kept up the pressure, demanding with loud voices that He be crucified. And their voices won out.

The next part of your journey to *Switching Systems* is to understand the principle of applying pressure. The passage above teaches us that there is power in pressure. Verse 23 highlights how the crowd would not let up. This behavior led to them receiving their request. Hear me closely and listen with your good ear. The accomplishment of your dreams and desires requires pressure. If you want it, put pressure on it. If you desire it, put pressure on it. If you envision it, put pressure on it. Whatever your it is, it will demand an application of pressure.

To take it a step further, we must also learn how to put pressure on God. For a few, I could feel you tense up and squirm in your seat. But do not throw the book out the window or your tablet under the sofa. Let's look at Scripture.

Matthew 7:11 says, *If you then, being evil, know how to give good gifts to your children, how much more will your Father who is in heaven give good things to those who ask Him!*

Applying pressure is not a reflection of our arrogance, instead it demonstrates our trust in God's abundance. Because of the finished work of Jesus on the cross, we have

God has the power, and pressure releases it!

access to a benevolent father. Therefore, asking God to get involved is an act of faith, not selfish ambition. It shows our dependence on Him and allegiance to Him. Putting pressure on God calls Jehovah into action and gives our spiritual superhero an opportunity to put on his cape! God has the power, and pressure releases it!

If you are like me, you like a good episode from Law & Order, Chicago P.D. or C.S.I. Miami. It is a common occurrence on one of these shows to see someone get shot. As tension rises and emotions escalate, we're left wondering if the person will survive. With urgency and purpose, the paramedics arrive on the scene. Upon approaching the victim and evaluating the wound, they immediately begin to apply pressure. They understand the application of pressure can cause the bleeding to stop.

With that image in mind, ask yourself, "Where am I bleeding?" Then ask yourself, "Have I applied pressure?" Similar to the victims in the show, your bleeding can be stopped. But this will require the intentional application of pressure to your wound. Let's look at a familiar bible passage to further illustrate this point.

Mark 5:25-34 (HCSB) says:

A woman suffering from bleeding for 12 years had endured much under many doctors. She had spent everything she had and was not helped at all. On the contrary, she became worse. Having heard about Jesus, she came behind Him in the crowd and touched His robe. For she said, "If I can just touch His robes, I'll be made well!" Instantly her flow of blood ceased, and she sensed in her body that she was cured of her affliction.

At once Jesus realized in Himself that power had gone out from Him. He turned around in the crowd and said, "Who touched My robes?" His disciples said to Him, "You see the crowd pressing against You, and You say, 'Who touched Me?'" So He was looking around to see who had done this. Then the woman, knowing what had happened to her, came with fear and trembling, fell down before Him, and told Him the whole truth. "Daughter," He said to her, "your faith has made you well. Go in peace and be free from your affliction."

Pressure is what made the difference for this woman. She applied pressure and virtue was released to cure her issue. Pressure has a way of getting you noticed. Pressure has a way of getting your needs addressed. Jesus sensed something different in this woman's

> As you put pressure on God, He puts pressure on your problem.

touch. Others surrounded Him, but this woman put pressure on what was in Him.

Many people in corporate America say, "The squeaky wheel gets the grease." How squeaky have you been lately? If you want to see a move of God, turn up the pressure. As you put pressure on God, He puts pressure on your problem.

A few ways to amplify spiritual pressure are through prayer, praise, agreement and confession. When used properly and consistently, these disciplines can dramatically change the results of your life. Make a commitment to yourself to intensify your focus and consistency in these four areas. Trust me. Your life will be better as God responds and takes notice of your efforts.

Low Tire Alert

Recently, I was driving and noticed the low tire pressure alert on my dashboard. Although thankful for the information, I was busy and did not take heed. After a few days of ignoring the signal, I noticed a change in the ride of the vehicle. I even recognized a decrease in fuel efficiency. These issues pushed me to make my way to the local tire shop to have the situation evaluated.

While sitting in the lobby of the automobile shop, Holy Spirit said to me, "Just like the car alerted you to a pressure issue, I have been signaling the body of Christ. The pressure is low!"

I find it amazing how God will use common occurrences to teach spiritual principles. Right there in the tire shop, my heart was moved to repent. I had allowed the function and ride of my life to be negatively impacted by low pressure.

I want to challenge you to honestly reflect at this moment. Is your low-pressure light on? Has Holy Spirit been signaling you to stop and address an issue? Do not allow the ride of your life to be hampered by ignoring the alert of God. Take heed before the enemy takes hold!

As important as it is to *apply* pressure, it is just as critical to *maintain* pressure. I heard Bishop I.V. Hilliard say recently in a sermon, "It is the cumulative effect of your prayer life that makes the difference." The keyword in that sentence is *cumulative*. It is the idea of continuity. We must build upon what's already been done. Applying pressure in our relationship with God is not a one-time occurrence. It's a daily habit.

Let's use an example from the business world and stock market to illustrate the point. Investing works when done consistently and regularly. You select stocks and pick mutual funds based on past performance. You increase the value of your portfolio by habitually putting money in over time. The goal is to receive a maximum return on your investment. But even better, the magic of the stock market is in something called compound interest. This is the idea that not only what you put in grows, but the growth also grows. With compound interest, your initial investment and your growth exponentially multiply. This allows you to amass wealth quicker as your money works harder.

Prayer, praise, confession and agreement are investments. They always deliver a return. The longer you do them, the more they work. The more you put in, the more value they create. I declare compounding is about to take place in your life. As prayer, praise, confession and agreement build up, multiplication is about to hit your life. Get ready to go faster, see more and encounter increase in the portfolio of your life.

Pressure Predators

Building pressure is one thing. But we must also be aware of leaks that can eradicate pressure. I call them pressure predators. There are four of them I want to bring to your attention: sin, disobedience, procrastination and pessimism. These silent enemies have the ability to cancel out the progress we are working so diligently to achieve.

Hebrews 12:1 (KJV) says, *"Wherefore seeing we also are compassed about with so great a cloud of witnesses, let us lay aside every weight, and the sin which doth so easily beset us, and let us run with patience the race that is set before us."*

The goal is to run a winning race for God. But the predator of sin is constantly at work against us. The enemy wants to impede our progress and create headwinds to forward advancement. Therefore, we must purposefully and strategically dismiss our sinful habits. Letting go of sin empowers us to maintain pressure.

With sin out of the way, we can address our next pressure predator: disobedience. We spoke earlier about how obedience is a component of the formula for abundance. But on the other hand, disobedience is a variable in the formula for lack. Obedience moves God toward us, while disobedience creates distance and separation from the Father. Complying with God is paramount if we want to maintain pressure. As Pastor Miranda Faye Pope says, "Agree with God. He's always right."

> If disobedience is not showing up, procrastination is being late.

Our next pressure predator is procrastination. As believers, we are oftentimes mindful and aware of what we *should* do. However, we cease to *act* promptly, and we lack a sense of urgency. I call procrastination delayed action. If disobedience is not showing up, procrastination is being late. It is important to understand timing in our faith walk. For some opportunities, being late is just as bad as not showing up at all. In both cases, you can end up empty-handed. Therefore, when God speaks, it is imperative to move quickly.

Finally, we must deal with the pressure predator called pessimism. Pessimism is released through the negative, failure-minded voices we allow to speak over us. If not careful, we will allow these voices to override God. If we revisit Luke 23:13-23, we see the pessimist character trait in action. Pilate is trying to convince the crowd to *not* crucify Jesus. He is giving his perspective and attempting to offer an alternative. They want Jesus, but Pilate is suggesting Barabbas. Yet, the people were demanding and persuasive. They would only be satisfied with the crucifixion of Jesus.

Although we do not like their cause, we can learn from their behavior. The mob refused to settle. They did not allow an opposing opinion to change their conviction. Instead, they resolutely stood on what they wanted to happen. Like the mob, do not allow anyone to talk you out of what you want.

Frequently, we settle for less than we want because we are tired of what we have. We routinely are the recipients of average because we did not have the fortitude to fight for great. I implore you to not accept less when you know God is able to do more. As we prepare to close this chapter, let's go back to where we began.

Luke 23:23 (HCSB) says, *"But they kept up the pressure, demanding with loud voices that He be crucified. And their voices won out."*

To demand means to ask authoritatively. It means to make an insistent request, made as if by right. In this verse, the crowd and Pilate knew someone had to be released due to the laws of the festival. Pilate tried to give them Jesus, but they demanded Barabbas. We know the people are confused based on who they chose. But God can still teach us something in their foolishness. The crowd didn't settle for what Pilate wanted them to have. They knew their rights and based their request off what was legally available. The people raised their voices and made a demand. Learn from the mob in Luke 23. Stop being passive. Open your mouth and make some demands to God based off your rights as a kingdom citizen. If the Word says you can have it, put pressure on God and demand it. Get bold with it! Get loud with it! Say what you want and say what God said!

When you know the law, and who wrote it, you have a justifiable right to demand what the law says. Whenever you read the Word, read it like a legal document. This approach

... your victory is in your voice!

places power in your hands to get results. You talk to God and reference His Word as support for your demand. God is a God of principles and promises. He is not a genie. When we know His principles and promises, we can call Him into action to shift outcomes in our favor.

You must realize your victory is in your voice! You possibly have been saying, "I am waiting on God to move." He said, "I have been waiting on you to talk!" In Luke 23, the crowd shouted, "Crucify him!" However, you need to say, "Heal me! Provide for me! Protect me! Preserve me! Expand me! Increase me! Multiply me! Shield me! Teach me! Show me!" Now is the time to open your mouth and win with your voice!

For some, opening your mouth and speaking makes you uneasy. I dare you to rise above that fear. Do not allow anxiety to extinguish your hopes. Fear shouldn't make you silent. The pain and traumatic experiences you have experienced are real. But you must fight back and choose not to succumb to the tragedy of your past. God is looking for you to raise your voice again. I want you to overcome yesterday and conquer today. This is the time to shift the results in your life and change the trajectory of your bloodline. Get your confidence back and reclaim your swagger. It all starts and ends with the words that come out of your mouth.

You are not dead. You are still alive. The fight is not over, and I feel another round on the horizon. Therefore, open your mouth, raise your voice and let a roar out. Psalm 107:6

(HCSB) says, *"Then they cried out to the LORD in their trouble, and he delivered them from their distress."* Your deliverance is in your voice. Do not allow trouble to mute you. Choose to call out to God and apply pressure.

What do you want God to do? Get it in your mind, release it out of your mouth, and watch God produce it in your life.

Pressure Pays Off

Luke 23:24-25 (HCSB) says, *So Pilate decided to grant their demand and released the one they were asking for, who had been thrown into prison for rebellion and murder. But he handed Jesus over to their will.*

> ... things break when pressure is applied!

I pray God grants your request in response to the pressure you apply. I pray God releases what you have been asking for. Whatever your desire is, it can be done. Be confident and stand in faith knowing things break when pressure is applied!

Flipping The Switch

>>>————◆◆◆ · · ◆ · · ◆◆◆————<<<

Switching systems is not automatic. It's an act of our will, and it requires our permission. Since the beginning, God has given man volition. Volition is defined as the power to use one's will to make choices, decisions and determinations. From the Garden of Eden to today, God has not and will not violate our will. God will present an opportunity, but we must decide to take advantage of it. God is sovereign; yet, He relates to us based off our choices.

The Word in 2 Peter 3:9 (HCSB) says, "*The Lord does not delay His promise, as some understand delay, but is patient with you, not wanting any to perish but all to come to repentance.*" It is the undeniable will of God that everyone would be saved. But although it is God's will that all would be saved, everyone will not be saved. Salvation requires a *choice* to accept Jesus Christ as our Lord and savior. We get to choose!

Romans 10:9-10 (HCSB) says, *If you confess with your mouth, "Jesus is Lord," and believe in your heart that*

*God raised Him from the dead, you will be saved. One
believes with the heart, resulting in righteousness, and
one confesses with the mouth, resulting in salvation.*

The key word in that passage is *you.* If you confess with
your mouth, and if *you* believe in *your* heart, salvation is
available. However, it requires your willful involvement.
Similarly, switching systems is not going to happen just
because God wants you to switch systems. Flipping the
switch will be the result of your choice to leave the world's
way and adopt the King's way. Switching systems will
require giving God permission to lead, rule and work on
your behalf.

Recently, I had a conversation with a group of people,
including my parents. In this dialogue, we discussed the
inflated price of Air Jordan gym shoes. I said, "I've never had
a pair of Air Jordan shoes. The acquisition cost is so high."

My mother quickly interjected and said, "You never had a
pair because you never asked for them." In that moment, I
realized that my absence of Air Jordan's was not because
my parents lacked the resources or ability to make it
happen. It was because I never asked them. So, I didn't have
Air Jordan's because I never gave my
parents the permission to act on my
behalf. How many times do we as
believers do the same thing? We go

> Every God
> addition
> requires man's
> permission.

without because we never give God permission to get involved. We never ask!

So, with this in mind, let's settle the debate once and for all. Every God addition requires man's permission. God can do it, but we must let Him. If we are going to experience increase, abundance, overflow, healing, prosperity, joy, peace, fulfillment and satisfaction, it will require our consent and authorization. The switch from living in the world's system to operating in heaven's system begins with a decision.

> Deuteronomy 30:19-20 (NLT) says, *"I call heaven and earth as witnesses against you today that I have set before you life and death, blessing and curse. Choose life so that you and your descendants may live, love the Lord your God, obey Him, and remain faithful to Him. For He is your life, and He will prolong your life in the land the Lord swore to give to your fathers Abraham, Isaac, and Jacob."*

The power to live is housed in the decisions you make. We have to *choose life*. As we choose life, it will require action. You never choose and remain stationary. You do not decide and stand still. Our decisions trigger movement. The movement and action are steps of faith. They serve as an expression of trust. Our actions signal which system we put our trust in. Let's examine a passage of Old Testament Scripture to see this principle at work.

Joshua 24:14-24 (NLT) says, "*So fear the Lord and serve him wholeheartedly. Put away forever the idols your ancestors worshiped when they lived beyond the Euphrates River and in Egypt. Serve the Lord alone. But if you refuse to serve the Lord, then choose today whom you will serve. Would you prefer the gods your ancestors served beyond the Euphrates? Or will it be the gods of the Amorites in whose land you now live? But as for me and my family, we will serve the Lord.*"

The people replied, "We would never abandon the Lord and serve other gods. For the Lord our God is the one who rescued us and our ancestors from slavery in the land of Egypt. He performed mighty miracles before our very eyes. As we traveled through the wilderness among our enemies, he preserved us. It was the Lord who drove out the Amorites and the other nations living here in the land. So we, too, will serve the Lord, for he alone is our God." Then Joshua warned the people, "You are not able to serve the Lord, for he is a holy and jealous God. He will not forgive your rebellion and your sins. If you abandon the Lord and serve other gods, he will turn against you and destroy you, even though he has been so good to you." But the people answered Joshua, "No, we will serve the Lord!" "You are a witness to your own decision," Joshua said. "You have chosen to serve the Lord." "Yes," they replied, "we are witnesses to what we have said." "All right then," Joshua said, "destroy the idols among you, and turn your hearts to the Lord, the God of Israel." The people said to Joshua, "We will serve the Lord our God. We will obey him alone."

In this passage, we see Joshua calling the people of God to the proverbial carpet. He is provoking them to decide who they will serve. Joshua is urging them to choose which system they are going to live in. He even leads by example and makes it clear which system he has chosen. But what arrests my thinking is how adamant Joshua is regarding them making the decision for themselves. He does not want the choice to come from pressure or manipulation. Instead, Joshua wants them to own their choice. Then, after making the decision, he calls them to act. He requests they destroy the idols they have in their possession.

> Compromise is not completely wrong; it is just not completely right.

This narrative provides a framework for how God wants to interact with His people. He wants us to choose, then own our choices. Once we decide, the next step is action.

However, as we act, we must not allow compromise to cost us our conquest! Compromise is not completely wrong;

it is just not completely right. It is partially accurate with a hint of error. This is where the enemy works overtime against believers. The adversary moves in the area of deception, and it gives birth to compromise. Many believers think that because they are doing certain things right, the small areas they are missing don't matter. But this is not biblical nor spiritually sensible.

> Song of Solomon 2:15 (NLT) says, *Catch all the foxes, those little foxes, before they ruin the vineyard of love, for the grapevines are blossoming!*

> Proverbs 14:8 (KJV) says, *"The wisdom of the prudent is to give thought to their ways, but the folly of fools is deception."*

> Colossians 2:8 NIV says, *"See to it that no one takes you captive through hollow and deceptive philosophy, which depends on human tradition and the elemental spiritual forces of this world rather than on Christ."*

> The Word in 1 Peter 5:8 (NKJV) says, *"Be sober, be vigilant; because your adversary the devil walks about like a roaring lion, seeking whom he may devour."*

These passages protect our faith from the enemy called compromise. They call us to consider our ways to safeguard them from deception. Additionally, the Word of God compels us to not place our trust in the systems of this world. Instead, it emphasizes finding our strength and power from Jehovah God. Finally, 1 Peter 5:8 specifically speaks to the opportunistic nature of the devil. He is scouting the earth for prospects for deception. If a person can be deceived, he or she can be a victim of compromise. Compromise will move you from being a conqueror to being conquered!

Stay woke, my friend!

Notes & Reflections

Put God In The Game

*G*od does not need our power, but He does require our partnership. It is a waste of opportunity and potential to get saved, then leave God on the bench.

> God does not need our power, but He does require our partnership.

It is time to maximize the partnership we have with Yahweh and unleash His power on our situations.

Put God in the game! To cement the point in your heart, consider a professional sports franchise. God is the owner. We are the coach. Holy Spirit is our star player. Although the owner supplies the roster, the coach must manage it. It is the responsibility of the coach to appropriately utilize and maximize their talent. The onus is on the coach to call the right plays, make timely substitutions, and position the team to win.

As the coach, we have to develop the game plan for our lives and use Holy Spirit to deliver victory. In athletic contests, whenever a substitution is made, a horn is blown. This alerts all parties that a new participant is entering the game. As I pen these words, I hear a horn sounding in the spirit realm. Now is the time to look down at the bench and tell Holy Spirit, "Check in!"

Let the enemy know a substitution is being made. Holy Spirit is entering the game of your life, and the momentum is about to shift in your favor.

Switching Mindsets

Recently, I attended a Purpose Bootcamp with Dr. Dharius Daniels. While participating in this intensive, God downloaded a revelation in my spirit. It was this: *You are afraid of the blessings God wants to give you*! You may be shocked to read that. I was just as shocked to hear it. Holy Spirit confronted my insecurities. He informed me that I was afraid of what God could do! Many of us trust God is able, but we question whether we qualify.

> You are not scared of the enemy as much as you are scared of yourself.

What do you do when possibility makes you nervous and potential makes you anxious? Some of us are afraid of what and who we are! You are not scared of the enemy as much as you are scared of yourself. It's your destiny that's intimidating you. The Promised Land is intimidating to you. Let's review a common biblical passage to show you how this can be possible.

Numbers 13:26-33 (Holman Christian Standard Bible) says:

The men went back to Moses, Aaron, and the entire Israelite community in the Wilderness of Paran at Kadesh. They brought back a report for them and the whole community, and they showed them the fruit of the land. They reported to Moses: "We went into the land where you sent us. Indeed it is flowing with milk and honey, and here is some of its fruit. However, the people living in the land are strong, and the cities are large and fortified. We also saw the descendants of Anak there. The Amalekites are living in the land of the Negev; the Hittites, Jebusites, and Amorites live in the hill country; and the Canaanites live by the sea and along the Jordan."

Then Caleb quieted the people in the presence of Moses and said, "We must go up and take possession of the land because we can certainly conquer it!"

But the men who had gone up with him responded, "We can't go up against the people because they are stronger than we are!" So they gave a negative report to the Israelites about the land they had scouted: "The land we passed through to explore is one that devours its inhabitants, and all the people we saw in it are men of great size. We even saw the Nephilim[e] there—the descendants of Anak come from the Nephilim! To

ourselves we seemed like grasshoppers, and we must
have seemed the same to them."

In this passage, we see something called The Grasshopper Complex. The spies could not deny the land had everything God promised. God's Word was true, but the spies questioned their readiness. They go as far as to call themselves grasshoppers. Even more disheartening is the assumptions they made. In verse thirty-three, they say, "*… and we must have seemed the same to them.*" How could the spies know what they were thinking? This is the danger of The Grasshopper Complex. You create false narratives in your mind and project them on others. But The Grasshopper Complex has to go. God is sending you to a place that is

> Think yourself
> somewhere
> different.

made for giants because you are a giant. Therefore, the fear of winning must go, in Jesus' name! God has more that He wants to give you. You have to shift your mindset from maintaining to expansion! As Dr. Daniels frequently says, "You go to the next level headfirst." Think yourself somewhere different.

Shifting mindsets is not for the faint of heart. It actually is a battle. The enemy does not want you to go higher. He doesn't want you to experience more. Therefore, he wages war in our minds and strategically deploys ambushes to stunt our forward advancement. His goal is to convince us to live beneath God's preferred and promised plan. This is why Scripture encourages us to perform a quality check on our minds. As believers, we have to ensure our thoughts line up with God's Word. We have to adopt the mind of Christ, a sound mind.

Philippians 2:5 (KJV) says, *"Let this mind be in you, which was also in Christ Jesus."*

The Holman Christian Standard Bible says it this way: *"Make your own attitude that of Christ Jesus."*

Both of these translations demonstrate the personal responsibility that rests with us to manage our mental outlook. God will help, but we have to take ownership. We have to think about what we are thinking about. The goal as a believer is for our mindset and attitude to reflect Jesus.

Areas To Shift Your Mind

*P*hilippians 2:3-8 (NLT) says, *Don't be selfish; don't try to impress others. Be humble, thinking of others as better than yourselves. Don't look out only for your own interests, but take an interest in others. You must have the same attitude that Christ Jesus had. Though he was God, he did not think of equality with God as something to cling to. Instead, he gave up his divine privileges; he took the humble position of a slave and was born as a human being. When he appeared in human form, he humbled himself in obedience to God and died a criminal's death on a cross.*

One of the areas we must shift our mind in is our thought process towards humility. The previous Bible passage clearly pinpoints the humility Christ walked in. I point this out as a concept we must embrace as believers and followers of Jesus. Jesus' example shows us that, in a world of self-promotion, the kingdom way is to be mindful of others. Our existence in the earth is to the glory of God and the advancement of humanity. The achievement of this mission requires us to adopt a humble approach and sacrifice. What are you willing to give up in order to go up?

The Word in 1 Peter 5:6 HCSB says, *Humble yourselves, therefore, under the mighty hand of God, so that He may exalt you at the proper time.*

The next mindset we must address is our attitude toward forgiveness. Romans 12:19 (NIV) says, *"Do not repay anyone evil for evil. Be careful to do what is right in the eyes of everyone. If it is possible, as far as it depends on you, live at peace with everyone. Do not take revenge, my dear friends, but leave room for God's wrath, for it is written: "It is mine to avenge; I will repay," says the Lord.*

So often, we want to take matters into our own hands. However, the Word offers an alternative approach: *peace*! Scripture teaches us to leave space for God to handle people and situations. We often block the move of God because our hands and our offense are in the way. But today, I am praying that you forgive whoever has wronged you so you can receive your release. Leave room for God!

> Forgiveness is not easy, but it is biblical.

I know a few of you took a big gulp when I said forgive the people that wronged and mistreated you. Trust me. I know it's difficult. Forgiveness is not easy, but it is biblical. We are recipients of forgiveness. Therefore, we should offer that same grace and mercy to others. Yes, this even includes our enemies. In the model prayer, Jesus teaches the disciples to pray they be forgiven of their trespasses as they forgive those who trespass against them. We must realize our own need for forgiveness. From that place, we will have the compassion and capacity to offer forgiveness to someone else.

Luke 6:27-36 (NLT) says:

"But to you who are willing to listen, I say, love your enemies! Do good to those who hate you. Bless those who curse you. Pray for those who hurt you. If someone slaps you on one cheek, offer the other cheek also. If someone demands your coat, offer your shirt also. Give to anyone who asks; and when things are taken away from you, don't try to get them back. Do to others as you would like them to do to you.

"If you love only those who love you, why should you get credit for that? Even sinners love those who love them! And if you do good only to those who do good to you, why should you get credit? Even sinners do that much! And if you lend money only to those who can repay you, why should you get credit? Even sinners will lend to other sinners for a full return.

"Love your enemies! Do good to them. Lend to them without expecting to be repaid. Then your reward from

heaven will be very great, and you will truly be acting as children of the Most High, for he is kind to those who are unthankful and wicked. You must be compassionate, just as your Father is compassionate.

The preceding passage challenges us not just to forgive, but to shift our mindset toward our enemies. We thank God for our friends, and it is easy to love them. But even when you don't do anything wrong, you will have enemies. When this inevitable occurrence happens, God has a way to handle these contentious situations and the participating individuals. It's simple: Love your enemies because, what you want, they can't give! They may have hurt you, and you want to harm them. I urge you to take a step back and breathe. Remember, your heavenly reward is not worth earthly retribution.

Luke 6:35 (NLT) says, *"Love your enemies! Do good to them. Lend to them without expecting to be repaid. Then your reward from heaven will be very great, and you will truly be acting as children of the Most High, for he is kind to those who are unthankful and wicked.*

God is kind because He does not repay people on the level of their offense. God deals with us and our offenders with a level of mercy and gentleness that is not deserved. This

> Release your enemies into the hands of a loving God who does not play about you!

is why the common cliché, "Kill them with kindness!" has biblical undertones. You could respond one way, but the kindness of God does more damage than the weapons of man. Release your enemies into the hands of a loving God who does not play about you!

Another mindset shift we must encounter involves generosity. God cannot be God of our lives if He is not Lord over our finances. Therefore, our attitude toward God's resources and the stewardship of them matters. Our financial stewardship will always dictate how blessed we are. The crops and harvests we have directly reflect our heart. If we are generous, God responds to that with abundance. If we are stingy, God blocks the flow of increase to us. God mirrors our mindset in relation to resources and harvest. Let's consult Scripture to see this principle clearly.

In 2 Corinthians 9:6-8 (NLT), the Word says:

Remember this—a farmer who plants only a few seeds will get a small crop. But the one who plants generously will get a generous crop. You must each decide in your heart how much to give. And don't give reluctantly or in response to pressure. "For God loves a person who gives cheerfully." And God will generously provide all you need. Then you will always have everything you need and plenty left over to share with others.

Money is not the most important thing. However, it is an answer to the most important things. If you need information or an education, money allows you to access it. If you catch a case, money will allow you to secure the lawyer to defend you. If you are struck with infirmity and disease, money will give you access to proper healthcare. In the kingdom of God, we do not chase money. However, we do realize the power it gives to help us live well and be kingdom financiers.

I am challenging you today to become a sower. If you are a sower, God will not only generously provide all you need—He will exceed it. Declare this: I got what I need, and I have plenty left over. Plenty, abundance and overflow are all adjectives to describe the life of a believer who sows.

> Revelation is revenue. Every thought is a check. Every idea is a stream.

When we are generous, God allows us to live out of both hands. We no longer become enslaved to any place, job or occupation. Instead, God opens our eyes to how our talents can create and produce wealth in various sectors of society. Having multiple streams of income is the will of God for His children. Revelation is revenue. Every thought is a check. Every idea is a stream. I pray as you read these pages that God releases divine ideas to you!

Mark 9:23 (NLT) says:

"What do you mean, 'If I can'?" Jesus asked. "Anything is possible if a person believes."

Mark 9:23 (HCSB) says:

Then Jesus said to him, "'If You can'? Everything is possible to the one who believes."

Mark 9:23 (AMP) says it this way:

Jesus said to him, "[You say to Me,] 'If You can?' All things are possible for the one who believes and trusts [in Me]!"

I offer multiple translations of this Scripture—not to be repetitive—but to emphasize opportunity. One of the final frontiers of shifting your mindset is adjusting your thoughts toward what's possible.

Anything and everything is possible to the person who believes. You set your belief level. You determine what you desire. You determine what is plausible. You have to take the stance that, "If God said it, I believe it." Scripture is backing you up and you have a word from God to stand on.

As you shift systems, it is essential to recognize you are not just changing your mind about God. You are actually changing your mind about *yourself.* You have a right to change your mind. In fact, I would suggest it is time to change your mind. The mindsets that have brought you to this point are not the ones you need to advance to the next place. God, through these pages, is stretching your thinking and aggravating your spirit. He wants you to know you can have more, do more and become more. But this requires a switch in systems and a change in your mindset.

For most vehicles, mechanics and dealerships recommend an oil change every 3,000 miles. This maintenance is necessary because, over time, the car has been exposed to different elements. These harmful particles can get into the oil in the engine and impact the car's ability to perform optimally. Therefore, the oil change is designed to cleanse the car of old oil and totally replace it with brand new oil. The old oil is not good for the future. Similarly, certain thoughts that were good for your past are not suitable for where you are going. Just like we have to change the oil in our car, we must *change the thoughts in our mind*. This allows us to perform at peak capacity, without breaking down.

As you peruse these pages, I pray God gives you a dream that makes your mind expand. I pray God would place a vision inside of you that creates a Holy discontent with your current situation. This does not mean you are ungrateful for all God has done. Neither does it mean you lose appreciation for what He has provided. It just means you have entered a mind space where you believe God can do more. Dreams signify that you are no longer content and satisfied with the status quo. You see more! You want more! You are in pursuit of more! God's dreams stretch us to a place mentally, emotionally and spiritually where we cannot return to the old. A new thing is coming, and it is now.

Isaiah 43:19 (NLT) says, *Behold, I will do a new thing; now it shall spring forth; shall ye not know it? I will even make a way in the wilderness, and rivers in the desert.*

Prepare yourself. Dreams are coming. God's dreams for you are being released. You are about to be exposed to a life you never knew existed. God's dreams are going to create opportunity where there was opposition and a path forward where you thought you were stuck.

Notes & Reflections

Switching Systems Requires Spiritual Maturity

><>━━━━━••◆ • • ◆ • • • ◆•••━━━━<<

*A*s we continue our journey in *Switching Systems*, it is imperative to pause for a moment. This switch is not automatic; it's a process. It will require commitment, perseverance and maturity. Maturity is a powerful word and worthy of us unpacking. The Merriam-Webster dictionary defines maturity as reflecting growth, development and being ripe for use. These phrases pack incredible potency for transforming our walk with God. Switching systems requires us to grow up. We must develop beyond our current state and get to a place where we are ripe for the Master's use. When we reach this place of completion, that is when supernatural exploits take place.

> Joshua 6:1-5 says, *Now Jericho was strongly fortified because of the Israelites—no one leaving or entering. The Lord said to Joshua, "Look, I have handed Jericho, its king, and its fighting men over to you. March around the city with all the men of war, circling the city one time. Do this for six days. Have seven priests carry*

seven ram's-horn trumpets in front of the ark. But on the seventh day, march around the city seven times, while the priests blow the trumpets. When there is a prolonged blast of the horn and you hear its sound, have all the people give a mighty shout. Then the city wall will collapse, and the people will advance, each man straight ahead."

This familiar biblical passage highlights the power of maturity. Joshua told the Israelites to walk around the wall once per day for six days. On the seventh day, they were instructed to walk around seven times. The interesting yet often overlooked component of this story is they cannot talk.

Joshua 6:10 says, *"Joshua commanded the people: "Do not shout or let your voice be heard. Don't let one word come out of your mouth until the time I say, 'Shout!' Then you are to shout."*

I can only imagine the difficulty of keeping so many people quiet. We can all remember how challenging it was for our elementary school teacher to quiet the class. Consider how difficult it had to be to quiet a nation. But through Joshua's leadership, and the people's compliance, they were able to exercise maturity. This maturity became the foundation for their victory. Listen closely, my friend. Victory follows maturity. We cannot go up if we never grow up.

Switching systems requires spiritual maturity to walk around your wall, see it still standing, and keep coming back until it falls. These are the testing moments that separate winners from losers. This is the place where the mature leaders rise to the occasion while the infantile fade to the background. In these defining moments, switching systems requires perseverance and the tenacity to keep obeying God even when it looks like nothing is happening. I urge you to embrace and demonstrate maturity. Do not get frustrated when you don't see progress with your natural eye. Do not get fatigued and quit because it seems as if your efforts are not producing results. Keep following the instructions, even when it doesn't look like it's working.

The wall cannot withstand God's instructions. The obstacles may be formidable, and the opposition may seem daunting. But, stay in faith. What you are facing cannot survive the instructions God gave you. The enemy wants you to cave under pressure and be intimidated by the  wall. But, look to 1 Corinthians 15:58 (NLT) for direction and support:

So, my dear brothers and sisters, be strong and immovable. Always work enthusiastically for the Lord, for you know that nothing you do for the Lord is ever useless.

Walking is our responsibility. The wall is God's responsibility. God simply asks us for obedience, and He handles the outcome. You walk! Let God handle the wall!

If you can be mature and embrace this process, the Word of the Lord for you is, "It will break!" I don't know how it's going to break. I'm not sure when it's going to break. I don't know who God will use or the time of their arrival. But based off Scripture, we can have confidence that the wall will come down.

> The Word of God says in 1 John 5:14-15 (HCSB): *"Now this is the confidence we have before Him: Whenever we ask anything according to His will, He hears us. And if we know that He hears whatever we ask, we know that we have what we have asked Him for."*

> The Message Translation says, *"How bold and free we then become in his presence, freely asking according to his will, sure that he's listening. And if we're confident that he's listening, we know that what we've asked for is as good as ours."*

The wall has to come down. The hold has to break. The situation has to change. Do not throw away your confidence as it carries a great reward. Simply believe God, maintain your hope, and trust God to bring down the wall. I sense it breaking in your life, and I dare you to receive it by faith!

The Posture of The Mature

>»»————•••◆ · · · ◆ · · · ◆•••————«<«

*A*fter reading the last section, you may feel a deeper accountability for growing up. Now, let's center ourselves on what we should be doing as we seek to grow toward spiritual maturity. One key ingredient to the recipe for maturity is worship.

I know that seems like a completely different topic. However, worship is a discipline we must adopt. Worship is not a 15–20-minute segment in our church services. It is not dictated by the tempo of a song. Worship truly expresses the heart's posture and position. Worship takes the focus and responsibility off of us and places it squarely on the shoulders of Jesus. Strong's Concordance defines worship as: an active response to the character, words and actions of God, initiated by His revelation and enabled by His redemption, whereby the mind is transformed, the heart is renewed, and actions are surrendered—all in accordance with His will and in order to declare His infinite worthiness.

... worship while we wait!

This definition of worship pushes us to a deeper place. We go beyond words and the motions to a place of surrender. Worship allows us to be in awe of God while He works on us. As we cultivate and nurture a life of maturity, we must learn to *worship while we wait*! While you wait on the breakthrough, worship. While you wait on the wayward child to return, worship. While you wait for the diagnosis to change, worship. While you wait on the resources and business deal to manifest, worship. While you wait for the wall to come down, worship! Worship reminds God that we still see Him as Lord. The wall may be standing in front of us, but it's temporary. We can lift our hands and voices. We can celebrate with expectation because we know the wall won't be standing for long.

> Philippians 2:10-11 (NLT) says, "*... that at the name of Jesus every knee should bow, of things in heaven, and things in earth, and things under the earth; and that every tongue should confess that Jesus Christ is Lord, to the glory of God the Father.*"

> Romans 14:11 (HCSB) says, "*It is written, As I live,*" saith the Lord, "*every knee shall bow to me, and every tongue shall confess and give praise to God.*" *Your wall will not get the last laugh. It will bow. Just keep your bend.*

Worship and Impatience

*W*orship calms the spirit of anxiety and helps us navigate impatience. This is critical as we frequently move too fast. Can you look back over your life and see where rushing birthed disobedience? Can you reflect upon a time where you wanted "there" more than you wanted Him? Can we be honest and say, at points, we wanted it and not God? It happens to us all. But this moment provides an opportunity to re-focus and recalibrate. In worship, we can re-discover God's pace!

Don't get ahead of God! Wait! Incomplete is the result of impatience. We never want to arrive at our destination underdeveloped or prematurely. That's why waiting is so important. The wait allows our timing to be synchronized with God's perfect plan and will. Here are some Scriptures to help us hit the brakes and stay in the timing of God:

Psalm 27:14 (HCSB)

Wait for the Lord; be strong and courageous. Wait for the Lord.

Psalm 37:7 (HCSB)

Be silent before the Lord and wait expectantly for Him; do not be agitated by one who prospers in his way, by the man who carries out evil plans.

Proverbs 20:22 (HCSB)

Don't say, "I will avenge this evil!" Wait on the Lord, and He will rescue you.

Isaiah 25:9 (HCSB)

On that day it will be said, "Look, this is our God; we have waited for Him, and He has saved us. This is the Lord; we have waited for Him. Let us rejoice and be glad in His salvation."

Wonderful things come to those who wait. Your wait is going to pay off. Raise your expectations and heighten your anticipation. God is working on it while He is working on you.

Switching Languages

long this journey, we have learned the benefits of applying pressure, switching systems, switching sources, and shifting our mindset. Now, it's time to switch languages. Language and words are the matter through which life is created.

> Hebrews 11:3 (KJV) says, *Through faith we understand that the worlds were framed by the word of God, so that things which are seen were not made of things which do appear.*

> Proverbs 18:21 (HCSB) says, *Life and death are in the power of the tongue, and those who love it will eat its fruit.*

We cannot ignore language and think we will inherit God's promises. Let's take a look at a few powerful excerpts from legendary philosophers regarding language.

Ludwig Wittgenstein said, "The limits of my language mean the limits of my world."

Federico Fellini said, "A different language is a different vision of life."

Cesar Chavez said, "Language is a reflection of the growth and character of its speaker."

Rita Mae Brown said, "Language is the roadmap of a culture. It tells you where its people come from and where they are going."

Language can liberate or hinder. It can break barriers or create ceilings. When used correctly, language allows people to break free from captivity and explore new realms of opportunity. But when used incorrectly, language creates prisons that confine the human soul and spirit. God wants to address our language because He wants to remove our limitations.

Language is a gift that gives you the chance to create a different vision for your life and an upgraded version of yourself. Wherever you are, you do not have to stay there. Your language can literally produce a new life for you. You are never stuck if you can still open your mouth.

My mother has a classic saying: "Better for people to think you are a fool than for you to open your mouth and remove all doubt." Language reveals our growth, development and character. Luke 6:45 KJV says, … *for out of the abundance of the heart the mouth speaks.* Our language and words shine a light on our inner man. It reveals where we have advanced, but it also identifies where we still have opportunities for improvement. Our character is exposed through our language. Our words show who we are. God wants to shift our identity and values, one word at a time.

> Isaiah 55:11 HCSB says, *"...so My word that comes from My mouth will not return to Me empty, but it will accomplish what I please and will prosper in what I send it to do."*

> The Amplified translation says it this way: *"So will My word be which goes out of My mouth; It will not return to Me void (useless, without result), Without accomplishing what I desire, And without succeeding in the matter for which I sent it."*

> The New Living Translation says, *"It is the same with my word. I send it out, and it always produces fruit. It will accomplish all I want it to, and it will prosper everywhere I send it."*

When we speak God's Word, we forfeit participating in empty seasons. The Word fills voids. It delivers results. The Word of God always accomplishes its goals and hits its target. The Word of God prospers in us. The Word is actually a seed that produces fruit. Therefore, as we align our language with the Word, we shift our world.

Joshua 1:8 (NLT) says, "*Study this Book of Instruction continually. Meditate on it day and night so you will be sure to obey everything written in it. Only then will you prosper and succeed in all you do.*"

God's language changes us, then we change the world.

Rita Mae Brown's quote from above packs an incredible punch. She uncovers the concept that language has reflective and prospective characteristics. It can be used to understand where a person has come from. At the same time, it can be used to highlight where someone is headed.

As kingdom citizens, we are apart of a kingdom culture. Heaven has a language. Learning this language and using it provides respect for our history and context for our future. Now is the time to stop using a language that does not define who you are or where you are headed. Switch languages.

First Peter 2:9 (NLT) tells us, "*... for you are a chosen people. You are royal priests, a holy nation, God's very own possession. As a result, you can show others the goodness of God, for he called you out of the darkness into his wonderful light.*"

As royalty in Christ, our lifestyle and our language should reflect whose we are and the kingdom we are a part of.

Get An Interpreter

$\rangle\!\rangle\!\!\rightarrow\!\!\leftarrow\!\!\rightarrow\!\!\bullet\quad\cdot\cdot\bullet\cdot\cdot\quad\bullet\!\!\rightarrow\!\!\leftarrow\!\!\leftarrow$

*G*od desires to expand your language so He can expand His kingdom. As we seek to fully adopt God's system, we must comprehend that the audience determines the language. If you were in Spain, you would speak Spanish. If in Italy, you would speak Italian. If in France, you would speak French. If in the hood, you would speak Ebonics! This concept may seem elementary, but it uncovers a revelation worth exploring. Where you are determines what language you use. This thought is monumental as it demonstrates the requirement to be flexible. The variety and diversity of your language determines the difference and impact you can make.

Every audience is different. Every audience requires a specific language for understanding to occur. We see this in Scripture in Acts 2 on the day of Pentecost. Each person heard it in their own language. This speaks to the strategy and foresight of God. God doesn't want language barriers in the kingdom. The Gospel is limitless in its reach and scope if we align the right language with the right audience.

> You can have oil yet lack the language to distribute it!

It is possible to communicate, and the audience doesn't comprehend because they do not speak the same language. You can be anointed yet have a language barrier. You can have oil yet lack the language to distribute it! Recently, I was watching a PGA golf tournament where Hideki Matsuyama won. Of course, the media wanted to interview Hideki and discuss his achievement. But there was a slight problem. Hideki is a Japanese golfer who is fluent in Japanese. He doesn't speak English. Although he could speak Japanese, the audience listening, and the reporter interviewing him, spoke another language. Therefore, his competence in Japanese did him no good in the current interview. The audience demanded a language he did not have mastery in. With this example as a backdrop, take a moment and reflect over the next two questions. How many times have we found ourselves in situations that demanded a language we did not have proficiency in? Can you remember a time when you were speaking, yet you felt as if the audience didn't understand or respond?

Hideki knew he had a language gap. He realized a communication barrier stood in the way of him and his audience. Therefore, an interpreter accompanied him. He knew he had something to say, and he strategically aligned a resource to assist him. This interpreter helped him overcome his communication hurdle. Similarly, God has given us something to say and people to affect. This requires a language adjustment and a communications assistant. We call him Holy Spirit.

> The Word in 1 Corinthians 2:11 (HCSB) says, *"For who among men knows the thoughts of a man except the spirit of the man that is in him? In the same way, no one knows the thoughts of God except the Spirit of God."*

> The New Living Translation says it this way: *"No one can know a person's thoughts except that person's own spirit, and no one can know God's thoughts except God's own Spirit."*

As we journey through life, we have to learn how to let the Holy Ghost interpret. Based on the Scriptures we read, Holy Spirit knows the thoughts of God. He is intimately acquainted with what God is doing and how He is moving. If we allow Holy Spirit to give us God's thoughts, words and language, we will see dramatically different results.

Now, we understand that our audience determines the language. Additionally, we see the importance of Holy Spirit being our interpreter. The next step is to acknowledge that our future location demands language training. You have to learn how to talk like where you are going to be! If you were to take a job abroad, you would have to learn the language of your future residency. The location of your existence would demand a certain level of language proficiency. You would learn the language of the land where you are going to live and work. Similarly, God is taking you to a new place. Therefore, He is teaching you the language of your next destination. There is a promised land God plans to dispatch you to eventually. Your occupancy of this place requires a certain language. I urge you to develop the language of where you are headed. What does prosperity sound like? What is the language of peace, joy and love? Wherever you want to be, start talking like it *now*!

Language shifts living! You have to alter your language if you are going to adjust your lifestyle. The next level of living is found in the Word of God.

Colossians 3:3 (NLT) says, *"For you died to this life, your real life is hidden with Christ in God."*

As we spend time with Jesus, we learn the language of conquerors, champions and winners. The secret to next level living is hiding in the Bible. Open it, find you, and find the language of your next. Our words have the power to shape experiences and create possibilities. Genesis 1  highlighted the ability that is housed in the right language. God used words to create a world that existed in His mind. God thought, God spoke, and the world was formed.

Similarly, since we are created in the image of God, we have the grace to create with our words. Your next level of living is waiting on your speaking to evolve. You cannot live a *big* life using *small* words.

Your tongue is the doorway to your future! It is a key that unlocks opportunities and uncovers fresh experiences. Use your key. Do not live a limited life when God has given you limitless potential through His Word. God's Word is a language that creates a better future. If you want your life to be better tomorrow, start speaking heaven's language today.

A major component in language development is relationships. We will discuss this more comprehensively later. But let me quickly unpack how your relationships and surroundings organically teach you how to speak. Think of a child. They learn the language of their parents based on proximity. Who the child is around determines what language the child will speak. The child mimics the sounds and words they have been exposed to at home and other familiar places. Similarly, as spiritual children, we adopt the language of our environment. We embrace and recite the words of those we trust and live with. Since this is the case, we have to intentionally study and expose ourselves to the language of the level we desire.

Although Scripture is the primary source of language for the believer, we must not minimize the benefit in studying the language of people we want to be like. Whatever you want to be, someone already is. Find them, study their language, and begin to become what they already are. Dr. Dave Martin shared a powerful philosophy regarding people and language on his podcast. He said, "Whenever you meet someone, ask them: What do you know that I need to know?" The premise of the question is the idea that each person holds invaluable treasure inside of them. If we take a moment, we can tap into who they are and what they know. This allows us to develop from their experiences and receive wisdom from their life challenges. In the words of Bishop I. V. Hilliard, "A friend is someone whose heart you trust, but a mentor is someone whose wisdom you trust."

Wisdom is all around us. Information is readily available. Answers are hidden in the people God sends to your life. If we can be sensitive and aware, we can tap into a language that will shift our entire existence. God seeks to transform your life forever and it begins with a "fresh" word. I pray for you that God would give you the language and words to possess what your heart desires. I am in faith with you that your language will undergo a massive renovation and lead to an upgraded life.

Hide-and-Seek

$\rightarrow\!\!\!-\!\!\bullet\cdots\blacklozenge\cdots\bullet\!-\!\!\!\leftarrow$

*W*hen I was a kid, my brothers and I played hide-and-seek. This classic childhood game involved one group going to hide while a blindfolded person counted. Then, the blindfolded individual would say, "Ready or not, here I come!" The person would remove the blindfold and go search for the hidden participants. Of course, if you were found and tagged, you became "it." Oh, what memories I have trying to locate my brothers.

As I ponder that childhood game, I see a correlation to our life as believers. Many of us have gone a variety of places and the Word of God has to find us. The Word seeks us out and pulls us from our place of seclusion and isolation. We see this happening in Scripture in the life of a man named Jeremiah. Let's explore his story for a moment to discover the powerful locating ability of God's Word.

Jeremiah 1:4-10 (HCSB) says:

The word of the Lord came to me: "I chose you before I formed you in the womb; I set you apart before you were born. I appointed you a prophet to the nations." But I protested, "Oh no, Lord, God! Look, I don't know how to speak since I am only a youth." Then the Lord said to me: "Do not say, 'I am only a youth,' for you will go to everyone I send you to and speak whatever I tell you. Do not be afraid of anyone, for I will be with you to deliver you. This is the Lord's declaration." Then the Lord reached out His hand, touched my mouth, and told me: "I have now filled your mouth with My words. See, I have appointed you today over nations and kingdoms to uproot and tear down, to destroy and demolish, to build and plant."

Notice how the story opens. It begins with, "The word of the Lord came to me." Jeremiah did not find God's Word. Instead, like hide-and-seek, God's Word found Jeremiah. Similarly, I declare the Word of the Lord is about to find you! In the midst of your obscurity, the Word is going to find you. In the middle of your seclusion, the Word is about to locate you. Even in your isolation, the Word of the Lord is going to come to you.

When the Word of the Lord arrives, it is going to spark a transformation. Get ready to be tagged by the life-giving, life-changing Word of God. When you receive God's Word, it changes your person, your purpose for living, and your plans. Like Jeremiah, the Word of the Lord comes to clearly

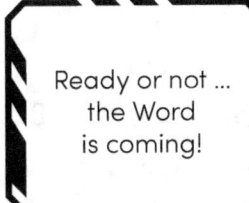

Ready or not ... the Word is coming!

identify who you are. This is critical as many people live decades without discovering their raison d'être, or their reason for existence. But God's plans for you are clear and intentional. His Word reveals His heart for you. The father does not want you to wander aimlessly. Ready or not ... the Word is coming!

As we dig further into this text, we see Jeremiah protesting the Word of the Lord. Jeremiah says, "Not me Lord!" If I were to imagine how this conversation flowed, I can hear Jeremiah saying, "You got the wrong person, God." Can you relate to this experience? Have you ever protested the Word of the Lord concerning you? If so, I have been sent to tell you to stop the protest!

Say, "Yes!" to God and His plan for your life! I know it can be overwhelming to consider. I understand it can be intimidating to comprehend. Although your natural man may be shaking in your boots, remember that your spirit is willing and capable. Receive the word! It's not too big. It's not too much. It's not out of your reach. It's possible. Anything is possible to the one who believes. Not only *can* God do it for you; He *wants* to do it for you!

In Jeremiah 1:6-7, Jeremiah speaks about being too young to do what God called him to do. Interestingly enough, God does not correct Jeremiah. He does not deny the fact that Jeremiah is a youth. Instead, he tells Jeremiah not to say that he is young. What Jeremiah was saying was a fact. But the facts were about to block God's plan for Jeremiah's life. So often, we stop the power of God from moving by stating facts. I'm not saying live in denial. But I am saying do not allow the facts to detour your declarations and alter your faith in God's Word.

The facts say: broken, sick, disappointed, poor, overlooked and overwhelmed. You are right in your observation. However, take a step back and believe that God is right about you, too. God's thoughts of you are higher and bigger. His thoughts are going to change the facts. God's words are true, and that truth will make you free. God is changing your mind about *you*. He is freeing you from the facts and introducing you to the truth. You have been created to be, do and have so much more. Believe that to be true and start living like it.

Watch Your Mouth

*I*n Jeremiah 1:9-10, God reached out and touched Jeremiah's mouth. The almighty touched the lips of Jeremiah to fix his language. God filled him with the right words. It's possible to have the right thoughts in your head, yet the wrong words on your lips. It is possible to have the

> It's possible to have the right thoughts in your head, yet the wrong words on your lips.

right passion in your heart yet fail if your mouth is misaligned. Therefore, watch your mouth! In fact, you may need a word transfusion. Like Jeremiah, we may need a touch from God. This way, our mouths will be infused with the Word of God and bring life.

It is my hope that, as you read these pages, you sense God's power stirring within you. My goal isn't to give you goosebumps and all the feelings. Instead, my prayer is that God moves within you so a new language can come out of you. I decree that, like Jeremiah, God is about to touch your mouth. With the correct words, you can erase failure and step into success.

Success is not automatic. It requires your participation. God is not going to speak for you, but He will give you the words to speak! It is our responsibility to respond with the Word when situations arrive. God's Word will always precede the trials and tribulations that arise. God loves you so much that He gives you the answers to the test before you are examined. Our obligation is to study so we can recall the answers under pressure. Being able to remember and recite what God said will cause you to live the life God intended. Success is inevitable when God's Word collides with your unique dilemma.

Talk Your Way Out

*ow, I want to preface this next section by asking you not to judge me. Don't judge the pastor for the disclosure he is about to make. Here goes: *I have never been in a fight.* Yes, you heard right. From birth until now, I have never been in a physical fight. I have not thrown hands, let them fly, or had to knuck if you buck. When I share this with people in my life, they all look at me in disbelief. Some giggle as they prepare to take my hood credibility away from me. They frequently ask how it is even possible for me to have never been in a fight. It is then that I reveal to them my secret for avoiding having to exchange blows: *I talk myself out of everything!*

I am always observing, listening, and evaluating the situations I find myself in. Then, I seek to use the proper

> Wherever you are, talk your way out!

words to de-escalate arguments and reduce the probability that a fight ensues. That has been my strategy. Forty-three years later, it is still working. I share this personal example with you because you don't always have to fight to win. You can talk yourself into success and safety. God will give you the language to navigate all situations.

Wherever you are, talk your way out! Talk your way out of poverty. Talk your way out of sickness. Talk yourself out of relational discord. Talk yourself out of fear. Talk yourself out of hopelessness. My prayer for you is that God would give you the language of freedom. This language allows you to step out of bondage and into the life He promised.

You may ask, "How do I receive this language? How do I find the words to approach my current place in life?" Good questions. The way to receiving your language and word transfusion is dedicating consistent time in the presence of God. The more time we spend with Him, the more He talks to us. Your time with the Father is not always about what you tell Him. Rather, the most powerful moments are when He shares with you. God wants to bring you into His presence to give you a new language. God wants to prep you for your specific audience and mission. There are people you are supposed to touch and assignments you must complete. This requires the appropriate language. The time you spend basking and lingering in the presence of God creates the space and opportunity for God to release a download.

If you have an iPhone, it frequently sends updates to optimize the effectiveness of your device. But just because the update is available does not mean it is in operation on your device. You have to accept the terms of the update. You have to connect your phone to power. You have to make sure it is connected to the Wi-Fi network. Once this happens, the update is downloaded to your device. From this point, you can operate your device according to what the manufacturer has released for your enjoyment.

We have to follow a similar process to receive God's updates. We must accept His terms (God's will), connect to the power (Holy Spirit), and join heaven's network through praise and worship. If you follow this process, what's in the heavens will be downloaded to your life. Heaven's dream for you will become your reality. The goal is for the purpose of God to be fulfilled in earth through you. Based on Matthew 6:10, we decree, as it is in heaven, it will be in the earth.

As we close this section on language, I pray that you never sit in a room you do not have language for. As God elevates you to greater platforms, opportunities, and stages, may His language travel with you. May you possess the wisdom of God that is available to those who ask. I pray Psalm 19:14 will be your portion:

> "Let the words of my mouth, and the meditation of my heart, be acceptable in thy sight, O LORD, my strength, and my redeemer."

Your words and language are going to be from God. They will please God. Your switch in language is going to transform you and the lives of countless others!

Switch Relationships

>>―――――――・・・◆・・・―――――――<<

$\mathcal{W}$e have made amazing progress. So far, we have made the decision to switch systems. We have learned the criticality of applying pressure. We are changing and expanding our mindset. We are learning and being filled with a new language. Now, God is going to challenge you to switch your relationships.

> Proverbs 13:20 (HCSB) says, *The one who walks with the wise will become wise, but a companion of fools will suffer harm.*

> Proverbs 13:20 (AMP) says, *He who walks [as a companion] with wise men will be wise, But the companions of [conceited, dull-witted] fools [are fools themselves and] will experience harm.*

> The New Living Translation says, *Walk with the wise and become wise; associate with fools and get in trouble.*

Switching systems will require a shift in thought concerning those you do life with. As Dr. Daniels says, "It is impossible to get life right when we get relationships wrong." We cannot become what we do not associate with. However, what and who *we walk with will greatly determine our results in life and give a preview of our future.*

We replicate what we are exposed to. Find me a person concerned about their physical health, and I bet they are surrounded by those who value fitness. Think of the person invested in their spiritual development. You will most likely find them connected to other like-minded individuals who are full of faith. People focused on career advancement and business success associate with one another. Find me a man committed to honoring his wife and family, and you will see him sharing space with those who share his sentiments. This same concept applies to education, finance and ministry.

... you become what you connect to!

Here's the principle: you become what you connect to! You have to find it, then follow it. I am a firm believer that it's not *what* you have; it's *who* you have. Who you have in your life will lead you into what you need. Let's examine a biblical passage to further expound on this topic.

Luke 22:7-13 (HCSB) says,

Then the Day of Unleavened Bread came when the Passover lamb had to be sacrificed. Jesus sent Peter and John, saying, "Go and prepare the Passover meal for us, so we can eat it." "Where do You want us to prepare it?" they asked Him. "Listen," He said to them, "when you've entered the city, a man carrying a water jug will meet you. Follow him into the house he enters. Tell the owner of the house, 'The Teacher asks you, "Where is the guest room where I can eat the Passover with My disciples?"' Then he will show you a large, furnished room upstairs. Make the preparations there." So they went and found it just as He had told them, and they prepared the Passover.

This story clearly illustrates the power of following the right person. The disciples were sent to the city to prepare for Passover. Jesus told them to look for a man carrying a water jug. This was the man they were supposed to follow. This alone is insightful. Jesus did not tell them to just follow anyone. He told them to specifically follow the man carrying the water jug. Why? Because, who you follow will determine where you end up.

The man carrying the water jug led the disciples to the right place. But sadly, many people end up in the wrong place because they follow the wrong people. Who you follow will heavily influence if you see what Jesus promised. The disciples followed the man with the jug and he led them to the right place. Then, they were able to ask for what Jesus told them to ask for. The disciples' obedience and connection to the right individual led them to a large, furnished room. In this place, the disciples prepared for an encounter with Jesus.

God cares about who we associate with. There is territory we are called to possess and spaces we are destined to occupy. However, the right relationship is the key to gaining access. If the disciples never met the man with the jug, they would have never found the large, furnished upper room. Relationships are the key to unlocking what God has already prepared for you. God's greatest blessings come in the form of people and relationships. When you find your people, you have found the blessing. We were never meant to do life alone.

When God wants to bless you, He sends a person. When the enemy wants to curse you, he sends a person. People can be instrumental in our success or contribute to our failure. That is why selecting the proper circle is essential for winning in life. For many, the desire to keep the same crew is impeding their progress and affecting their future. But I pray God leads, guides and pushes you to new relationships, fresh blood and purposeful connections. I pray you find the man with the water jug so you can step into God's preferred future for you.

The Power of The Right People and The Right Words

>>>———••◆ · · ◆ · · · ◆••———+<<

enesis 11:1-7 (NLT) says:

At one time all the people of the world spoke the same language and used the same words. As the people migrated to the east, they found a plain in the land of Babylonia[a] and settled there. They began saying to each other, "Let's make bricks and harden them with fire." (In this region bricks were used instead of stone, and tar was used for mortar.) Then they said, "Come, let's build a great city for ourselves with a tower that reaches into the sky. This will make us famous and keep us from being scattered all over the world." But the Lord came down to look at the city and the tower the people were building. "Look!" he said. "The people are united, and they all speak the same language. After this, nothing they set out to do will be impossible for them! Come, let's go down and confuse the people with different languages. Then they won't be able to understand each other."

> There is power and limitless possibility when relationship and language work together.

The story of the Tower of Babel is an incredible example of the interplay between relationship and language. The people were united behind a vision. They shared a common goal. More importantly, they spoke the same language and used the same words. This combination of relationships and unified language allowed them to succeed in their efforts. There is power and limitless possibility when relationship and language work together.

Imagine what you could accomplish with the right people and the right words. God even says that nothing is impossible when you operate this way. You literally can achieve anything you set out to do! You tap into the supernatural and unlock miracles when you stand with other people of God. Now we see why the enemy works overtime to create confusion and misunderstanding in the body of Christ. Both of these demonic ploys can stop vision from happening. If the devil can create a misunderstanding, he can break the synergy in the relationship. When synergy and unity are impacted, the results suffer. So many projects have been halted because of disputes and disagreements. Many goals are left unfulfilled because people could not, or refuse to, navigate differences. But I pray this will not be your story. You will link up with the right people and maintain unity. As you do, you will do the impossible and build a life that glorifies God.

Notes & Reflections

Living by Believing

*W*ell family, we have made it to the end of our journey. As we close our time together, I want you to search your heart. It's time to decide. This is the moment you make your move. This is your opportunity to take your life, family, bloodline, business and future in a different direction. But this will require *faith*.

It takes faith to abandon our plan and follow God's plan, especially when we don't have all the details. It takes faith to switch systems! Moving forward, you will live by believing. Your decisions will be motivated by faith. Your choices will be rooted in the Word of God. Your total operating system for life is shifting to the kingdom of heaven. Switching Systems is about abandoning the natural realm and living on the promises of God, no matter what we see or hear. The next season of your life is about to be legendary. Your expectations have been stretched and now you realize more is possible. We respect sight, but we live by vision!

> We respect sight, but we live by vision!

The Word in 2 Corinthians 5:7 (HCSB) says, *For we walk by faith, not by sight.*

The New Living Translation says, *For we live by believing and not by seeing.*

The God's Word translation says, *Indeed, our lives are guided by faith, not by sight.*

Finally, the Amplified version says it this way: *For we walk by faith, not by sight [living our lives in a manner consistent with our confident belief in God's promises].*

A few years back, I had the opportunity to ride ATVs in the Mexican Riviera. As we showed up for the excursion, the host emphasized that we were in dangerous terrain. Therefore, it was imperative that we listen to the tour guide and follow his directions. We would be navigating the jungles of Mexico, and our safety was linked to our trust. We had to listen and follow our director's instructions if we wanted to enjoy the journey. Of course, the wild side of me wanted to venture out alone. But the voice of Holy Spirit pulled me back in. I had to realize my desire for exhilaration could cost me my life. So, I fell in line and had the time of my life following the leader.

Similarly, you are about to embark on a journey into the wild by faith. Holy Spirit is your tour guide to the life God planned for you. You will be tempted to go off on your own.

Don't do it. Stay with the guide. Follow the leader. He knows the way and your safety is His top priority. The ride will not only be safer, but it will be better when you let Holy Spirit lead the way.

Now let me warn you of one of the dangers lurking in the wild jungle of faith. It's called frustration. As you switch systems, you will want to see instant results. But oftentimes, you will encounter what looks like delay. The enemy, at moments, will amplify the intensity and frequency of the attacks against you. He hopes to convince you that, if it's not happened, then it won't happen. If you are not careful, frustration will tempt you to take matters into your own hands and revert back to the old way. But I urge you to not allow delays to pressure you into taking a detour. You may be on a diet, and the weight is not coming off. Keep eating right and exercising. You may be budgeting, and it still seems like the debt is not being erased. Stay with it. You started tithing, and the car broke down and the refrigerator stopped working. Do not change course. You enrolled in school and now you feel overwhelmed balancing home and class. Stay focused. Things may feel harder, but be encouraged, they are getting better. Embrace the suck and stick with your new system. A new life is on the horizon if you just don't give up.

Galatians 6:9 (NLT) says, *So let's not get tired of doing what is good. At just the right time we will reap a harvest of blessing if we don't give up.*

Psalm 37:23 (AMP) says, *The steps of a [good and righteous] man are directed and established by the LORD, And He delights in his way [and blesses his path].*

Stay the course! God is ordering and directing your steps. He is blessing your path! God has tailor-made blessings just for you. But they require that you follow His leading. Do not miss the blessing by detouring. Proverbs 14:12 says, *There is a way that seems right to a man, but the end is death.* Trust God's way and stick with His plan. You are going to arrive at a place called *more* because you dared to *switch systems.*

About The Author

›-›»————••◆ · · · ◆ · · · ◆•——————-«‹‹

Leon McDonald, III

$\mathcal{A}$s a pastor, thought leader, and agent of change, Leon McDonald, III understands that his greatest success doesn't come from his awards or accolades. It comes from helping others win in their personal and professional life as they pursue their God-given purpose. While many are consumed with their personal success and development, he's intentional about playing an integral role in the success and development of others. With over 30 years in ministry, and over 20 years in the marketplace, McDonald is a master at inspiring, empowering and equipping leaders to not only survive challenging times-but thrive through challenging times.

As a sales leader and marketing expert for Pfizer Inc., Leon has received numerous awards for delivering significant performance and revenue for the organization. Additionally, his leadership of The Winners Circle Church has impacted the community by delivering several outreach and philanthropic efforts to serve those in need. Holding a Bachelor of Communications Degree with a concentration in Pre-Med from Albion College, McDonald also received multiple awards for his academic and athletic achievements. Understanding that information and knowledge alone doesn't yield transformational change, he works diligently to impart wisdom into everyone he encounters so that their dream life becomes a reality.

In his second book, *Switching Systems*, McDonald takes readers on a journey of self-discovery and self-reflection as they change the way they think so they can change the way they live. Challenging readers to shift in the way they think, speak and act, he provides a strategic framework for living a victorious, fruitful life of intentionality. Knowing that many desire more out of life, career and family, he empowers readers to shift from the world's system to the kingdom system and following kingdom principles.

Notes & Reflections